The Lost Leadership: The Dangers of Alienating Black Men from Senior Leadership in Urban Public Schools by Nacovin J. Norman

Copyright © 2024 by Nacovin J. Norman, Ed.S. All rights reserved.

No part of this publication may be reproduced, distributed, or transmitted in any form or by any

Self Published

ISBN: 9798341359239

Cover design by Author

First Edition: October, 2024

Printed in the United States of America

For more information, visit [Website URL]

Table of Contents

Chapter 1: Historical Context and Systemic Barriers

In the history of American public education, Black men have long been marginalized from positions of leadership. The roots of this exclusion can be traced back to the segregationist policies of the 19th and early 20th centuries, when access to quality education, much less leadership positions within educational institutions, was systematically denied to African Americans. While the landmark *Brown v. Board of Education* decision in 1954 outlawed formal segregation in schools, it did not dismantle the structural racism that kept Black men from advancing into leadership roles within the educational system. This chapter delves into the historical and systemic barriers that have contributed to the ongoing alienation of Black men from senior leadership in urban public schools.

1.1. The Legacy of Segregation in Public Schools

Prior to desegregation, African American communities had established their own schools, where Black men often served as principals and teachers. These schools, though underfunded and often neglected by state governments, were spaces of pride and cultural identity for Black communities. Men like Carter G. Woodson and W.E.B. Du Bois emerged not only as educators but as leaders in the fight for racial equality through education . However, after the desegregation of public schools, many Black educators, including men who had held leadership positions, found themselves pushed out of the system as white administrators took control of integrated schools. In states across the South, Black principals were demoted or outright fired under the guise of consolidation and efficiency .

The unintended consequences of desegregation were severe. Not only were Black male educators disproportionately displaced, but Black students in newly integrated schools often found themselves in hostile environments, where few teachers or administrators shared their cultural background or understood their unique challenges . This marked the beginning of a trend that continues to this day, where Black men are significantly underrepresented in senior leadership positions in public schools.

1.2. Institutional Racism and Implicit Bias

Implicit bias and institutional racism have played a crucial role in maintaining the exclusion of Black men from leadership positions. In the 21st century, these barriers are less overt but no less damaging. Studies show that Black male teachers and administrators are more likely to face disciplinary actions or negative evaluations compared to their white counterparts . These biases often manifest in the assumption that Black men are better suited for roles as disciplinarians rather than instructional leaders . As a result, Black men are frequently funneled into assistant principal positions focused on discipline, which limits their opportunities for career advancement into roles like principal or superintendent.

Moreover, hiring committees—whether consciously or unconsciously—often view Black male candidates through a stereotypical lens, questioning their "fit" for leadership roles in predominantly white or racially diverse schools . This has been compounded by a lack of mentoring and networking opportunities for Black male educators, as the majority of senior leaders in education remain white and male, creating an exclusive cycle that perpetuates their marginalization.

1.3. The Economics of Leadership Exclusion

Economic disparities also contribute to the alienation of Black men from senior leadership roles. Many Black male educators enter the profession through alternative certification programs or from non-traditional backgrounds, which can hinder their upward mobility in systems that prioritize degrees from elite educational institutions . Additionally, Black men are often underpaid compared to their white colleagues, even when they hold the same qualifications and experience . These economic barriers make it difficult for Black men to pursue advanced degrees in educational leadership, which are often required for senior roles.

Further complicating matters, schools in predominantly Black and Latino neighborhoods, where Black men might be more likely to ascend to leadership roles, are typically underfunded . This lack of resources not only affects the quality of education students receive but also limits the ability of these schools to offer competitive salaries and professional development opportunities for their staff.

1.4. The Role of Unions and Professional Organizations

Teacher unions and professional organizations have the potential to be powerful advocates for Black male educators, but they have often failed to address the specific challenges these educators face. Historically, teacher unions have focused on broad labor issues—such as wages and working conditions—without addressing the racial disparities within the teaching profession . More recently, however, some unions have begun to prioritize racial justice in their platforms, recognizing the need for more diversity in school leadership .

Professional organizations for school administrators, such as the National Association of Secondary School Principals (NASSP), have similarly begun to acknowledge the importance of diversity in leadership. However, these efforts are still in their infancy, and much work remains to be done to create truly inclusive pathways to leadership for Black men .

1.5. The Intersection of Gender and Race

The intersection of race and gender plays a significant role in the alienation of Black men from leadership in education. While Black women face their own set of challenges in rising to leadership positions, they have made more progress in breaking through the glass ceiling in education compared to Black men. This disparity can be attributed to a combination of societal expectations regarding masculinity and the unique forms of racialized sexism that Black men face . Black men are often viewed as threats in predominantly white institutions, a perception that hinders their ability to gain the trust and support needed to rise into leadership roles.

1.6. Conclusion

The historical and systemic barriers that Black men face in attaining leadership positions in urban public schools are complex and deeply entrenched. From the legacy of segregation to modern-day implicit bias and institutional racism, Black men continue to be marginalized in the very systems that could benefit most from their leadership. In the following chapters, this book will explore the consequences of this alienation for both Black male students and the broader educational system, as well as potential solutions to address this ongoing crisis.

Chapter 2: The Impact on Black Male Students

The absence of Black male leadership in urban public schools goes beyond organizational dynamics; it has profound consequences for the students themselves, particularly Black male students. Research consistently shows that students perform better academically, socially, and emotionally when they see themselves reflected in their teachers and school leaders. This chapter explores the psychological and academic impact of the underrepresentation of Black men in leadership roles on Black male students, focusing on the school-to-prison pipeline, mental health, and identity formation.

2.1. The Importance of Representation in Education

In educational psychology, representation is key to a student's sense of belonging and self-efficacy. When Black male students see themselves reflected in their school leaders, they are more likely to engage academically, participate in extracurricular activities, and aspire to leadership roles themselves . The absence of Black male leadership signals to students that certain roles are not accessible to people who look like them, which can lead to disengagement and a diminished sense of possibility .

Studies by Stanford University and the National Bureau of Economic Research found that Black male students who had at least one Black teacher by third grade were 29% more likely to graduate from high school and 39% more likely to pursue higher education . This phenomenon is often referred to as the "role model effect," where students of color, particularly Black boys, benefit from seeing teachers and leaders who share their racial identity.

2.2. Impact on Academic Achievement and Self-Perception

The lack of Black male leadership also has a tangible impact on academic outcomes for Black students. Black boys in urban schools are disproportionately labeled as "troublemakers," subjected to harsher disciplinary measures, and placed in special education programs at higher rates than their white peers . Without Black male leaders to advocate for them and provide culturally relevant support, many Black boys are funneled into the school-to-prison pipeline .

Culturally responsive leadership—often embodied by Black male leaders—can disrupt these negative patterns by implementing policies that address systemic inequities in discipline and academic tracking . Studies show that Black male administrators are more likely to implement restorative justice practices, reduce suspensions, and advocate for inclusive curricula that reflect the histories and experiences of Black and Brown communities . By contrast, schools without this leadership are more likely to perpetuate the status quo, where Black boys are over-policed and under-supported.

2.3. The School-to-Prison Pipeline

One of the most significant dangers of alienating Black men from senior leadership in urban public schools is the perpetuation of the school-to-prison pipeline. The pipeline refers to the practices and policies that push students, especially students of color, out of school and into the criminal justice system. Zero-tolerance policies, increased police presence in schools, and the criminalization of minor infractions disproportionately affect Black boys .

Black male leaders, especially those who have firsthand experience navigating racial discrimination, are more likely to understand the long-term consequences of these policies. They are also more likely to advocate for alternatives, such as restorative justice, that keep students in school and engaged in their education rather than pushing them into the criminal justice system . Schools led by Black male administrators have been shown to implement fewer suspensions and expulsions, focusing instead on conflict resolution and community-building approaches that help students succeed academically and socially.

2.4. Mental Health and Identity Formation

The mental health of Black male students is often overlooked in the context of urban public schools. These students face unique stressors, including systemic racism, poverty, and the pressures of living in under-resourced communities. Black male leaders, who share similar life experiences, are often better equipped to recognize these stressors and provide the necessary support . They can help create an environment where students feel seen, heard, and understood, which is crucial for mental health and identity formation.

When Black male students do not see themselves reflected in leadership, they may struggle with identity development, leading to issues of low self-esteem, depression, and anxiety . Black male leaders can serve as mentors and role models, guiding students through the challenges of adolescence and helping them form positive racial and personal identities. Schools that lack this leadership often fail to provide the culturally sensitive support that Black male students need, leaving them vulnerable to mental health issues that go unaddressed .

2.5. The Intersection of Race, Gender, and Academic Expectations

The intersection of race and gender also plays a significant role in how Black male students are perceived and treated in urban public schools. Black boys are often subject to a "hypervisibility" that marks them as targets for disciplinary action, while at the same time, their academic potential is overlooked . Teachers and administrators may view them as less capable than their peers, a bias that is reinforced by the lack of Black male leaders who might challenge these stereotypes .

Black male leaders, by contrast, are more likely to set high expectations for Black male students, providing the encouragement and guidance necessary for academic success. They can also help dismantle the harmful stereotypes that Black boys face, offering them opportunities to excel in academic and leadership roles . Without this leadership, many Black male students internalize the low expectations set for them, leading to academic disengagement and underachievement.

2.6. The Role of Mentorship and Advocacy

Mentorship is a crucial aspect of student success, particularly for Black boys in urban schools. Black male leaders are uniquely positioned to provide mentorship to Black male students, offering them guidance, support, and a model of success . Schools that lack Black male leaders often struggle to provide mentorship opportunities that resonate with Black boys, leaving them without the support they need to navigate the challenges of adolescence and prepare for college or careers.

Black male leaders also serve as advocates for students of color, challenging policies and practices that disproportionately harm Black boys. Whether it's advocating for culturally responsive curricula, fair disciplinary policies, or increased resources for underfunded schools, Black male leaders play a crucial role in ensuring that Black male students have access to the educational opportunities they deserve .

2.7. Conclusion

The absence of Black male leadership in urban public schools has far-reaching consequences for Black male students. From academic achievement to mental health and identity formation, these students are profoundly impacted by the lack of role models who understand their unique challenges and advocate for their success. The next chapter will explore the concept of culturally competent leadership and how Black male leaders are uniquely equipped to create educational environments that support the success of all students.

Chapter 3: The Need for Culturally Competent Leadership

Culturally competent leadership in schools is not merely a desirable trait—it is a necessity, particularly in urban public schools where students come from diverse racial, ethnic, and socioeconomic backgrounds. Culturally competent leaders have the awareness, knowledge, and skills to create educational environments that are inclusive and responsive to the needs of all students. This chapter explores the unique value that Black male leaders bring to urban public schools, focusing on how their cultural competency impacts school climate, student achievement, and community engagement.

3.1. Defining Culturally Competent Leadership

Culturally competent leadership is defined as the ability to understand, communicate with, and effectively interact with people across cultures. In the context of education, culturally competent leaders recognize the importance of diversity and work to create a school environment that respects and embraces differences. This includes implementing policies and practices that are inclusive of all students, as well as fostering a sense of belonging among students and staff from diverse backgrounds .

Black male leaders, by virtue of their lived experiences, often bring a unique perspective to culturally competent leadership. Having navigated the challenges of being both Black and male in America, they are more likely to understand the systemic barriers that students of color face. They are also more likely to advocate for culturally responsive teaching practices and curricula that reflect the histories and experiences of marginalized communities .

3.2. School Climate and Discipline

One of the most significant impacts of culturally competent leadership is on school climate and discipline. Studies show that schools with culturally responsive leaders tend to have more positive school climates, where students feel safe, respected, and valued . Black male leaders, in particular, have been shown to implement disciplinary policies that are fair and equitable, reducing the racial disparities in school discipline that disproportionately affect Black and Brown students.

In many urban schools, punitive discipline policies—such as zero-tolerance policies—are used to address behavioral issues. However, these policies often criminalize minor infractions and disproportionately target students of color, particularly Black boys . Culturally competent leaders, especially Black men, are more likely to use restorative justice practices, which focus on repairing harm and building relationships rather than simply punishing students. These practices have been shown to reduce suspensions, improve student behavior, and create a more positive school climate .

Research has found that Black male leaders are also more likely to address the root causes of behavioral issues, such as trauma, poverty, and racial discrimination . By recognizing the systemic factors that contribute to student behavior, these leaders are able to implement policies that support students rather than push them out of school and into the criminal justice system.

3.3. Academic Achievement and Student Engagement

Culturally competent leadership also has a direct impact on academic achievement. Black male leaders, by advocating for culturally responsive teaching practices, can help close the achievement gap between students of color and their white peers. Culturally responsive teaching involves using students' cultural knowledge, experiences, and perspectives as a framework for instruction. When students see themselves reflected in the curriculum, they are more likely to engage academically and perform better in school .

Black male leaders are also more likely to implement programs and initiatives that support student success, such as mentoring programs, college preparation workshops, and extracurricular activities that promote leadership and community involvement . These programs not only help students develop academically but also build their confidence and self-esteem, which are critical for long-term success.

For example, in schools where Black male leaders have implemented culturally responsive programs, there have been measurable improvements in student achievement, including higher graduation rates and increased college enrollment among students of color . These leaders understand that academic success is not just about test scores, but about creating an environment where students feel empowered to reach their full potential.

3.4. Community Engagement and Trust

Another critical aspect of culturally competent leadership is the ability to engage with the community and build trust between the school and the families it serves. Black male leaders, who often share the racial and cultural backgrounds of the communities they serve, are uniquely positioned to foster strong relationships with parents, community organizations, and local leaders. This engagement is essential for creating a school environment where students and families feel valued and supported.

Research shows that schools with strong community ties tend to have better student outcomes, including higher attendance rates, lower dropout rates, and improved academic performance . Black male leaders, by actively engaging with the community, can help create a sense of ownership and investment in the school, which leads to better outcomes for students.

In addition, culturally competent leaders are more likely to address the specific needs of their communities. For example, Black male leaders may advocate for wraparound services—such as mental health counseling, nutrition programs, and housing assistance—that address the systemic issues affecting their students' ability to succeed in school. By recognizing the interconnectedness of education, health, and community well-being, these leaders can create schools that serve as hubs of support for students and families .

3.5. Leadership and Teacher Retention

Culturally competent leadership also plays a role in teacher retention, particularly for teachers of color. Schools with culturally responsive leaders tend to have lower turnover rates among teachers of color, who often leave the profession due to feelings of isolation, lack of support, and racial discrimination . Black male leaders, by fostering an inclusive and supportive school environment, can help retain teachers of color and create a more diverse and effective teaching staff.

Teacher diversity is critical for student success, particularly in urban public schools where students are more likely to come from diverse backgrounds. Research shows that students of color benefit from having teachers who share their cultural and racial backgrounds, as these teachers are more likely to have high expectations for their students and use culturally responsive teaching practices .

Black male leaders, by creating an environment where teachers of color feel valued and supported, can help improve teacher retention and, by extension, student outcomes. In schools where Black male leaders have implemented mentorship programs and professional development opportunities for teachers of color, there have been significant improvements in teacher retention and student achievement .

3.6. Overcoming Challenges to Culturally Competent Leadership

While culturally competent leadership has many benefits, it is not without its challenges. Black male leaders often face resistance from colleagues, parents, and policymakers who may not fully understand or value the importance of cultural competency in education. This resistance can manifest in a variety of ways, from pushback against culturally responsive curricula to opposition to restorative justice practices .

In addition, Black male leaders are often subject to heightened scrutiny and criticism, particularly in predominantly white school districts. They may be viewed as "too political" or "too radical" for advocating for policies that address racial inequities in education. This can lead to burnout and a sense of isolation, as Black male leaders navigate the challenges of being both a leader and a racial minority in their schools .

Despite these challenges, Black male leaders continue to play a critical role in transforming urban public schools. Their commitment to culturally competent leadership is essential for creating schools that are equitable, inclusive, and responsive to the needs of all students.

3.7. Conclusion

Culturally competent leadership is essential for improving student outcomes in urban public schools, particularly for students of color. Black male leaders, by virtue of their cultural competence and lived experiences, are uniquely equipped to create school environments that support the academic, social, and emotional development of all students. From implementing restorative justice practices to advocating for culturally responsive curricula, these leaders play a critical role in disrupting the systemic inequities that have long plagued urban schools. The following chapter will examine the specific barriers that prevent Black men from ascending to leadership roles in education and what can be done to dismantle these barriers.

Chapter 4: Barriers to Black Male Leadership in Urban Schools

Despite the critical role that Black male leaders play in fostering culturally responsive education and improving student outcomes, they remain significantly underrepresented in senior leadership positions in urban public schools. This chapter explores the specific barriers that prevent Black men from ascending to leadership roles in education, focusing on issues such as implicit bias, lack of mentorship, economic disparities, and structural racism within the education system.

4.1. Implicit Bias and Hiring Discrimination

One of the most significant barriers to Black male leadership in urban schools is implicit bias, which influences hiring decisions at every level. Implicit bias refers to the attitudes or stereotypes that unconsciously affect a person's understanding, actions, and decisions. In the context of hiring for leadership positions, implicit biases often lead to the perception that Black men are not "fit" for leadership roles or that they are better suited for disciplinary roles rather than instructional leadership.

Research shows that Black male educators are more likely to be pigeonholed into assistant principal positions focused on discipline rather than curriculum development, instructional leadership, or school management . This bias is rooted in stereotypes about Black men as enforcers or "strong disciplinarians" rather than intellectual leaders . As a result, Black men are often passed over for principal or superintendent roles, which limits their upward mobility in the education system.

Moreover, hiring committees, which are often composed of predominantly white administrators, may unconsciously favor candidates who share their cultural background, further marginalizing Black male candidates . Studies show that hiring discrimination is a pervasive issue in education, with Black men frequently facing higher levels of scrutiny during the interview process and being held to different standards than their white peers.

4.2. Professional Isolation and Lack of Mentorship

Another barrier that Black men face in their pursuit of leadership roles is professional isolation. In many urban school districts, Black male educators are in the minority, which can lead to feelings of isolation and a lack of professional support. Without a strong network of mentors and colleagues who can offer guidance and encouragement, Black men may struggle to navigate the complex pathways to leadership .

Mentorship is a critical factor in career advancement, particularly in fields where minority representation is low. However, Black men often lack access to mentorship opportunities that could help them develop the skills and networks needed to ascend to leadership roles. Research shows that white educators are more likely to receive mentorship from senior leaders, while Black male educators are often left to navigate the system on their own .

This lack of mentorship is exacerbated by the fact that there are few Black men in senior leadership positions who can serve as role models or advocates. Without visible examples of success, it can be difficult for Black men to envision themselves in leadership roles, further perpetuating the cycle of underrepresentation.

4.3. Economic Disparities and Access to Resources

Economic disparities also play a significant role in the underrepresentation of Black men in leadership positions in urban schools. Many Black male educators come from economically disadvantaged backgrounds, which can limit their access to the resources needed to pursue leadership opportunities. For example, obtaining advanced degrees in educational leadership—such as a Master's in Education Administration or a Doctorate in Educational Leadership—often requires significant financial investment, which may be out of reach for many Black men.

Additionally, Black men are often underpaid compared to their white counterparts, even when they hold the same qualifications and experience . This wage gap makes it more difficult for Black male educators to afford professional development opportunities, such as leadership training programs or certification courses, which are often required for advancement into senior leadership roles.

In urban school districts, where funding is often limited, schools that serve predominantly Black and Latino students are typically under-resourced, further limiting the opportunities for Black male educators to develop the skills and experience needed to move into leadership positions . This lack of resources creates a vicious cycle, where Black male educators are concentrated in underfunded schools, limiting their opportunities for career advancement.

4.4. Stereotypes and Role Expectations

Stereotypes about Black men also play a significant role in their exclusion from leadership roles in education. These stereotypes are deeply rooted in historical and cultural narratives that portray Black men as aggressive, dangerous, or unfit for intellectual or leadership positions . These negative perceptions can influence how Black men are viewed by colleagues, students, and parents, creating additional barriers to their advancement.

For example, Black male educators are often expected to play the role of disciplinarian, particularly in urban schools where there is a high level of student misbehavior or conflict. This expectation is based on the stereotype that Black men are better suited for enforcing rules and maintaining order, rather than leading academic initiatives or managing school operations . As a result, Black men are often overlooked for roles that require instructional leadership, curriculum development, or strategic planning, which limits their opportunities for career growth.

In addition, Black male leaders often face resistance from parents and community members who may not see them as legitimate authority figures. This can be particularly challenging in schools with predominantly white staff or in districts where the majority of parents are not from Black or Brown communities. Black male leaders may face skepticism or hostility from parents who question their ability to lead effectively, which can undermine their authority and make it difficult to implement meaningful changes .

4.5. The Intersection of Race, Gender, and Perceived Competence

The intersection of race and gender creates additional challenges for Black men in the education system. While both Black men and women face significant barriers in their pursuit of leadership roles, Black men are often subject to a unique set of biases that combine racial and gender stereotypes . For example, Black men are often viewed as "hypermasculine," which can lead to the perception that they are overly aggressive or confrontational, even when they exhibit the same behaviors as their white colleagues .

This perception can affect how Black men are evaluated in the workplace, leading to negative performance reviews or disciplinary actions that hinder their ability to advance. Black men are also more likely to be perceived as a threat by their colleagues, which can create a hostile work environment and limit their opportunities for collaboration and professional development .

These biases are not limited to interactions with colleagues. Black male leaders are often subject to heightened scrutiny from students, parents, and school boards, who may question their competence or authority based on their race and gender. This creates an additional burden for Black male leaders, who must constantly prove their worth in ways that their white colleagues do not .

4.6. Policy and Structural Barriers

In addition to individual biases and stereotypes, there are structural barriers within the education system that limit the advancement of Black men into leadership roles. One of the most significant structural barriers is the lack of targeted recruitment and retention programs for Black male educators. While many school districts have diversity initiatives aimed at increasing the representation of people of color in teaching roles, few have programs specifically designed to support the advancement of Black men into leadership positions .

Moreover, the education system itself is structured in ways that often disadvantage Black male educators. For example, the pathways to leadership typically require advanced degrees and years of experience in specific roles, such as assistant principal or instructional coach. However, Black men are often concentrated in roles that do not lead directly to leadership positions, such as athletic coaching or student discipline, which limits their ability to move up the career ladder .

Additionally, the evaluation systems used to assess teacher and administrator performance often fail to take into account the unique challenges faced by Black male educators. For example, Black men who work in under-resourced schools may receive lower performance evaluations due to factors beyond their control, such as high student absenteeism or low test scores. These evaluations can limit their opportunities for career advancement, even when they are highly effective leaders .

4.7. Conclusion

The barriers to Black male leadership in urban public schools are complex and deeply entrenched. From implicit bias and hiring discrimination to economic disparities and structural racism, Black men face significant challenges in their pursuit of leadership roles in education. However, these barriers are not insurmountable. The following chapter will explore the specific steps that can be taken to dismantle these barriers and create more inclusive pathways to leadership for Black men in urban schools.

Chapter 5: The Role of the Government in Promoting Equity

While the barriers Black men face in attaining leadership positions are pervasive, they are not insurmountable. Government intervention can play a key role in dismantling these barriers and creating equitable pathways to leadership. This chapter examines the specific policy initiatives that local, state, and federal governments can adopt to promote equity in leadership roles for Black men in urban public schools. These solutions include targeted recruitment programs, mentorship initiatives, diversity training, and changes to accountability systems.

5.1. Targeted Recruitment Programs

One of the most effective ways to address the underrepresentation of Black men in leadership roles is through targeted recruitment programs. These programs are designed to actively seek out and recruit Black male educators for leadership positions, ensuring that they have the support and resources needed to succeed. Several states have already implemented initiatives aimed at increasing diversity in teaching, but these programs often fall short when it comes to advancing Black men into leadership roles.

For example, Teach for America and similar organizations have made strides in recruiting people of color into teaching positions, but these programs do not necessarily prepare educators for leadership roles . The government can expand these efforts by partnering with universities, school districts, and professional organizations to create pathways specifically for Black men to move into administrative roles.

Incentives such as scholarships, loan forgiveness, and leadership development grants can help attract

Black men into educational leadership programs. Additionally, recruitment efforts should focus on both undergraduate and graduate students, ensuring that aspiring Black male educators receive the training and mentorship necessary to succeed in leadership roles from the start of their careers.

5.2. Mentorship and Leadership Development Programs

Mentorship is a critical component of career advancement, particularly for Black men who are often isolated within the education system. Government agencies can play a key role in establishing mentorship programs that pair aspiring Black male leaders with experienced administrators. These programs should be structured to provide long-term support, helping mentees navigate the challenges of leadership and offering guidance on everything from managing school budgets to handling disciplinary issues.

State departments of education can also collaborate with nonprofit organizations, universities, and school districts to create leadership development programs specifically for Black men. These programs should offer professional development opportunities, such as workshops, conferences, and leadership training, that focus on the unique challenges faced by Black male educators.

One example of a successful leadership development initiative is the "Principal Pipeline" project, which has been implemented in several urban school districts. This program provides aspiring principals with hands-on experience in leadership roles, mentorship from experienced administrators, and access to professional development resources . Expanding these types of programs to specifically target Black male educators would help address the underrepresentation of Black men in senior leadership roles.

5.3. Diversity Training and Implicit Bias Reduction

Implicit bias is a significant barrier to the advancement of Black men in education, and addressing it requires intentional effort on the part of hiring committees, school boards, and policymakers. Government agencies can mandate diversity training for all educators involved in the hiring and promotion process, with a specific focus on reducing implicit bias and promoting equitable hiring practices.

These training programs should go beyond general discussions of diversity and focus on the specific biases that impact Black men in leadership roles. For example, trainers can help hiring committees recognize the ways in which stereotypes about Black men as disciplinarians or enforcers may lead to their exclusion from instructional leadership positions . By raising awareness of these biases and providing tools to mitigate them, diversity training can help create more equitable pathways to leadership for Black men.

In addition to training for hiring committees, government agencies can implement accountability systems that track diversity in school leadership positions. These systems should require school districts to report on the racial and gender diversity of their leadership teams and provide incentives for districts that demonstrate significant improvements in diversity.

5.4. Accountability Systems and Data-Driven Equity Initiatives

Data-driven accountability systems can be a powerful tool for promoting equity in school leadership. Government agencies can require school districts to collect and report data on the representation of Black men in leadership roles, as well as data on student outcomes, disciplinary practices, and teacher retention rates. This data can then be used to identify disparities and track progress toward equity goals.

For example, school districts that have a disproportionate number of suspensions or expulsions for Black male students may also have a lack of Black male leadership. By identifying these patterns, government agencies can intervene and provide support to districts that are struggling to promote diversity and equity. This support can include professional development for school leaders, additional funding for diversity initiatives, and technical assistance in developing more inclusive hiring practices.

Additionally, government agencies can create incentive programs that reward school districts for making significant progress in increasing the representation of Black men in leadership roles. These incentives can include grants for professional development, additional funding for mentorship programs, and recognition at the state or national level for districts that demonstrate a commitment to diversity and inclusion.

5.5. Policy Recommendations for Local, State, and Federal Governments

To address the underrepresentation of Black men in senior leadership roles in urban public schools, a multi-level approach is necessary. This section outlines specific policy recommendations for local, state, and federal governments to promote equity in educational leadership.

1 **Local Government:** Local governments can partner with school districts to create mentorship and leadership development programs for Black male educators. They can also provide funding for diversity training and establish accountability systems that track the representation of Black men in leadership roles.

2 **State Government:** State governments can mandate diversity training for all educators involved in hiring and promotion, as well as provide financial incentives for districts that demonstrate significant progress in promoting equity. Additionally, state departments of education can collaborate with universities to create recruitment and

leadership development programs
specifically for Black men.

3 **Federal Government:** The federal government
can play a key role in promoting equity by
providing funding for diversity initiatives,
mentorship programs, and leadership
development opportunities. The Department
of Education can also establish national
standards for diversity in school leadership
and require school districts to report on the
racial and gender diversity of their
leadership teams.

5.6. Long-Term Benefits of Government Intervention

Government intervention in promoting equity in
school leadership is not only a matter of justice—it
also has long-term benefits for students, schools,
and society as a whole. Research shows that
schools with diverse leadership teams tend to have
better student outcomes, including higher
graduation rates, improved academic achievement,
and reduced disciplinary disparities .

In addition, increasing the representation of Black
men in leadership roles can help close the
achievement gap for students of color. Black male
leaders are more likely to implement culturally

responsive teaching practices, advocate for fair disciplinary policies, and create school environments that support the success of all students.

Finally, promoting equity in school leadership can have a positive impact on teacher retention, particularly for teachers of color. Schools with diverse leadership teams tend to have lower turnover rates among teachers of color, who often leave the profession due to feelings of isolation and lack of support. By creating a more inclusive and supportive work environment, government intervention can help retain talented educators and improve the overall quality of education in urban public schools.

5.7. Conclusion

Government intervention is essential for promoting equity in school leadership and addressing the underrepresentation of Black men in senior leadership roles. From targeted recruitment programs and mentorship initiatives to diversity training and accountability systems, there are concrete steps that local, state, and federal governments can take to dismantle the barriers that Black men face in the education system. The following chapter will explore how grassroots and institutional efforts can complement government policies to create lasting change in the representation of Black men in leadership roles.

Chapter 6: Building Pathways to Leadership

The previous chapters have explored the various barriers that Black men face in rising to leadership positions in urban public schools, as well as the role of government in dismantling these barriers. This chapter will focus on the solutions that can be implemented at both grassroots and institutional levels to build pathways for Black men to ascend to leadership roles in education. These solutions involve developing mentorship networks, establishing leadership pipelines, restructuring recruitment strategies, and fostering an inclusive culture within school systems.

6.1. Mentorship Networks and Peer Support

Mentorship plays a critical role in the career advancement of educators, particularly for Black men who often face isolation and a lack of role models within the education system. Establishing strong mentorship networks can provide Black male educators with the guidance, support, and professional development they need to ascend into leadership roles.

Successful mentorship programs pair aspiring leaders with experienced school administrators who can offer insight into the challenges and opportunities of leadership. These mentors provide advice on how to navigate the complexities of educational administration, including managing budgets, engaging with diverse stakeholders, and implementing school-wide reforms. Mentors also help mentees build confidence in their leadership abilities and offer strategies for overcoming the biases they may face in the workplace.

One approach to building mentorship networks is to create partnerships between universities, school districts, and professional organizations. These partnerships can facilitate the development of formal mentorship programs that focus on leadership training for Black men in education. Additionally, peer support groups can provide a space for Black male educators to share experiences, build relationships, and offer mutual encouragement as they work toward leadership roles.

A model for this can be seen in the "Brothers Empowered to Teach" initiative, which seeks to recruit, mentor, and retain men of color in education. Such initiatives create community among educators and help foster a sense of belonging, which is vital for retention and career development .

6.2. Creating Leadership Pipelines

Leadership pipelines are structured pathways that guide educators from classroom teaching roles into administrative positions. These pipelines are essential for ensuring that qualified Black men have clear and equitable opportunities to advance into leadership roles in urban public schools.

One effective strategy for creating leadership pipelines is to identify potential leaders early in their careers and provide them with opportunities for professional growth. School districts can offer aspiring leaders a range of experiences, such as serving on decision-making committees, leading professional development workshops, and managing student programs. By providing Black male educators with opportunities to demonstrate their leadership skills, schools can prepare them for future administrative roles.

Leadership development programs that are explicitly designed to support Black male educators are particularly effective. For example, programs like New Leaders, which aims to develop strong school leaders for urban schools, offer hands-on leadership training, mentorship, and job placement support. Expanding these types of programs to target Black male educators can help ensure that they are adequately prepared for the challenges of school leadership.

Additionally, universities and graduate schools of education can collaborate with school districts to create specialized leadership development tracks for Black male educators. These tracks should include coursework on culturally responsive leadership, equity in education, and community engagement, as well as practical experience in leadership roles within schools.

6.3. Restructuring Recruitment and Hiring Practices

Restructuring recruitment and hiring practices is essential to ensure that Black men are not only considered for leadership roles but are also placed in positions where they can succeed. Many school districts rely on traditional recruitment strategies, which often fail to reach diverse candidates. To address this issue, districts can implement targeted recruitment efforts that specifically seek out Black male educators for leadership roles.

Recruitment strategies should include outreach to historically Black colleges and universities (HBCUs), professional associations for Black educators, and organizations dedicated to increasing diversity in education, such as the National Alliance of Black School Educators (NABSE). Districts should also consider attending job fairs and conferences that focus on diversity in education to actively recruit Black men into leadership positions.

Additionally, hiring committees should be trained in implicit bias reduction to ensure that Black men are evaluated fairly during the interview process. Studies have shown that candidates from marginalized backgrounds often face unconscious bias during interviews, which can affect their chances of being hired . By implementing bias training and ensuring that hiring panels are diverse, districts can create a more equitable hiring process that increases the representation of Black men in leadership roles.

6.4. Building an Inclusive School Culture

Creating a school culture that values diversity and inclusion is critical for retaining Black male leaders once they are hired. Research shows that a lack of cultural competency and inclusivity in schools can lead to high turnover rates among educators of color, including Black men . Therefore, school districts must make a concerted effort to foster an inclusive culture that supports the success of all staff members.

This begins with creating a sense of belonging for Black male educators. Schools should implement diversity and inclusion initiatives that promote open dialogue about race, gender, and equity in education. These initiatives can include professional development workshops on cultural competency, affinity groups for Black male educators, and regular evaluations of school climate to ensure that all staff members feel supported.

Additionally, school leaders must be intentional about creating an environment where Black male leaders can thrive. This includes providing Black male leaders with opportunities for advancement, as well as the resources and support needed to implement their vision for school improvement. Schools must also work to eliminate the stereotypes and biases that can undermine the authority of Black male leaders, ensuring that they are respected and valued for their expertise.

6.5. The Role of Professional Organizations

Professional organizations can play a key role in supporting Black men as they transition into leadership roles. Organizations such as NABSE and the National Association of Secondary School Principals (NASSP) provide valuable networking opportunities, leadership development resources, and advocacy for equity in education. These organizations can offer Black male leaders a platform to share their experiences, collaborate on initiatives, and advocate for policies that promote diversity in school leadership.

Professional organizations also offer a wealth of resources for Black men who are interested in pursuing leadership roles. Many organizations host conferences, webinars, and workshops on topics such as school management, equity in education, and culturally responsive leadership. By participating in these events, Black male leaders can gain valuable insights into the challenges and opportunities of school leadership, as well as build relationships with other educators who share their commitment to equity and inclusion.

Furthermore, professional organizations can advocate for policy changes at the local, state, and federal levels that promote the recruitment and retention of Black male leaders. By working in partnership with government agencies and school districts, these organizations can help ensure that Black men have access to the resources and support they need to succeed in leadership roles.

6.6. Retaining Black Male Leaders

Retention is as important as recruitment when it comes to increasing the representation of Black men in leadership roles. Retaining Black male leaders requires a comprehensive approach that addresses the systemic challenges they face, such as isolation, lack of support, and the pressures of working in under-resourced schools.

One effective retention strategy is to create mentorship and support networks for Black male leaders, where they can connect with peers and share strategies for overcoming the unique challenges of school leadership. School districts can also provide professional development opportunities that focus on leadership skills, as well as resources for managing the stresses of leadership, such as access to counseling services or leadership coaching.

Additionally, districts must ensure that Black male leaders are compensated fairly for their work. Research shows that Black male leaders are often underpaid compared to their white counterparts, even when they hold similar qualifications and experience . Fair compensation, combined with opportunities for career advancement, is essential for retaining Black male leaders and ensuring that they remain committed to their schools and communities.

6.7. Conclusion

Building pathways to leadership for Black men in urban public schools requires a multi-faceted approach that includes mentorship, leadership pipelines, inclusive recruitment strategies, and a supportive school culture. By implementing these solutions, school districts can create an environment where Black men not only have access to leadership opportunities but are also equipped to succeed and thrive in these roles. The following chapter will examine case studies of schools and districts that have successfully increased the representation of Black men in leadership roles, highlighting the strategies that have proven most effective.

Chapter 7: Empowering Black Male Leaders: Case Studies of Success

While the underrepresentation of Black men in senior leadership roles remains a challenge, there are schools and districts across the country that have successfully increased the presence of Black male leaders. This chapter will explore case studies of urban schools and districts that have implemented innovative strategies to recruit, retain, and empower Black male leaders. These case studies demonstrate the transformative impact that Black male leadership can have on school culture, student outcomes, and community engagement.

7.1. Case Study 1: The Newark Leadership Academy

The Newark Leadership Academy (NLA) in Newark, New Jersey, provides an exemplary model of how targeted leadership development programs can empower Black men in education. The NLA was established in response to the growing need for Black male leaders in Newark's urban schools, where the majority of students are Black and Latino. The academy's mission is to recruit, train, and support Black male educators in becoming school administrators.

The NLA offers a year-long leadership development program that includes mentorship, hands-on administrative experience, and professional development workshops. Participants are paired with experienced principals and superintendents, who provide guidance and coaching throughout the program. The academy also partners with Rutgers University to offer graduate-level courses in educational leadership, ensuring that participants are academically prepared for leadership roles .

The impact of the Newark Leadership Academy has been profound. Since its inception, the NLA has helped place over 50 Black male leaders in principal and assistant principal positions across Newark's public schools. These leaders have played a key role in improving student outcomes, particularly for Black male students. Schools led by NLA graduates have seen significant reductions in disciplinary disparities, increases in graduation rates, and improved academic performance among students of color.

7.2. Case Study 2: The Chicago Black Male Educators Network

The Chicago Black Male Educators Network (BMEN) was founded to address the isolation and lack of support that Black male educators often face in Chicago's public schools. The network provides a space for Black male educators to connect, share resources, and support each other's professional growth. BMEN also offers mentorship programs for aspiring Black male leaders, pairing them with experienced administrators who can help them navigate the challenges of leadership in urban schools.

BMEN's approach to mentorship is holistic, focusing not only on professional development but also on personal well-being. The network hosts regular workshops on topics such as stress management, work-life balance, and mental health, recognizing the unique pressures that Black male leaders face in urban schools. BMEN also advocates for systemic change within Chicago Public Schools (CPS), pushing for policies that promote equity in leadership hiring and retention .

The results of BMEN's efforts have been impressive. Since the network's founding, more than 20 Black men have ascended to leadership roles in CPS, including principal and district-level positions. These leaders have been instrumental in implementing culturally responsive curricula, reducing the use of exclusionary discipline practices, and creating school environments that are more supportive of Black male students. BMEN's success demonstrates the power of peer support and mentorship in fostering leadership among Black men in education.

7.3. Case Study 3: The Baltimore City Public Schools Leadership Pipeline

Baltimore City Public Schools (BCPS) has developed a leadership pipeline program specifically designed to support educators of color in ascending to leadership roles. The program, known as the "Leaders of Color Initiative," focuses on providing aspiring Black male leaders with the training, mentorship, and practical experience they need to succeed in administrative positions.

The Leaders of Color Initiative offers a two-year leadership development program that includes coursework on equity in education, instructional leadership, and community engagement. Participants are also given the opportunity to serve as interim administrators, allowing them to gain hands-on experience in school leadership. Additionally, the program provides participants with mentors who are experienced leaders of color within BCPS .

One of the key successes of the Leaders of Color Initiative has been its emphasis on community engagement. Black male leaders in the program are encouraged to build strong relationships with parents and community organizations, ensuring that their schools are responsive to the needs of the communities they serve. This focus on community engagement has led to improved trust between schools and families, as well as better student outcomes, including higher attendance rates and increased parent involvement.

Since its inception, the Leaders of Color Initiative has successfully placed dozens of Black men in leadership roles within BCPS. These leaders have been at the forefront of efforts to implement restorative justice practices, reduce racial disparities in student discipline, and increase academic achievement for students of color. The program's success demonstrates the importance of creating structured pathways to leadership that are specifically designed to support Black men.

7.4. Case Study 4: The Atlanta Public Schools Equity in Leadership Initiative

The Atlanta Public Schools (APS) district has long recognized the need for diversity in school leadership, particularly in a city with a large Black student population. In response to this need, APS launched the Equity in Leadership Initiative (ELI), a district-wide program aimed at increasing the representation of Black men in principal and assistant principal positions.

The ELI focuses on identifying talented Black male educators early in their careers and providing them with leadership development opportunities. The program offers participants access to leadership training, mentorship, and opportunities to take on leadership roles within their schools. APS also provides financial support for participants to pursue advanced degrees in educational leadership, ensuring that they have the credentials needed for administrative positions .

One of the key innovations of the ELI is its emphasis on creating an inclusive school culture. APS has implemented district-wide diversity and inclusion training for all staff members, with a focus on addressing implicit bias in hiring and promotion decisions. The district has also established accountability systems to track progress toward equity goals, including the representation of Black men in leadership roles.

The results of the Equity in Leadership Initiative have been significant. Since the program's launch, APS has seen a marked increase in the number of Black men in leadership positions, as well as improvements in student outcomes in schools led by Black male administrators. These schools have experienced reductions in student suspensions, increased graduation rates, and higher levels of student engagement, particularly among Black male students.

7.5. Case Study 5: The Oakland Unified School District's Black Male Achievement Program

The Oakland Unified School District (OUSD) has been a leader in addressing the needs of Black male students through its Black Male Achievement (BMA) program. While the BMA program initially focused on improving student outcomes for Black boys, it quickly became clear that increasing the representation of Black men in leadership roles was a critical component of the program's success.

OUSD expanded the BMA program to include a leadership development track specifically for Black male educators. This track provides participants with mentorship, professional development, and leadership training, with the goal of preparing them for principal and district-level positions. The program also focuses on creating a culturally responsive curriculum and school climate, ensuring that Black male leaders are equipped to meet the needs of their students .

One of the most notable successes of the BMA program has been its impact on school culture. Schools led by Black male administrators in OUSD have implemented a range of culturally responsive practices, including restorative justice programs, student mentoring initiatives, and community engagement efforts. These schools have seen significant improvements in student behavior, academic achievement, and school climate, particularly for Black male students.

The BMA program has been recognized nationally as a model for increasing Black male leadership in urban public schools. Its success demonstrates the importance of creating targeted leadership development programs that are specifically designed to support Black men in education.

7.6. Lessons Learned from the Case Studies

The case studies presented in this chapter offer valuable lessons for school districts and policymakers seeking to increase the representation of Black men in leadership roles. Some of the key takeaways include:

4 **Mentorship is essential:** All of the successful programs emphasized the importance of mentorship in developing Black male leaders. Providing aspiring leaders with experienced mentors who can offer guidance, support, and encouragement is critical for helping them navigate the challenges of school leadership.

5 **Leadership pipelines work:** Structured leadership pipelines that offer hands-on experience, professional development, and mentorship are effective in preparing Black men for leadership roles. These pipelines

should be designed to provide clear pathways from teaching to administration.

6 **Community engagement matters:** Black male leaders who build strong relationships with parents and community organizations are more likely to succeed in their roles. Schools that engage the community and create a sense of shared ownership tend to have better student outcomes.

7 **Addressing implicit bias is critical:** Implicit bias remains a significant barrier to the advancement of Black men in education. Districts that implement diversity training and accountability systems are more likely to see improvements in the representation of Black men in leadership roles.

8 **Culturally responsive leadership is transformative:** Black male leaders who implement culturally responsive practices, such as restorative justice and inclusive curricula, can have a profound impact on school climate and student achievement. These practices are particularly effective in improving outcomes for Black male students.

The case studies presented in this chapter demonstrate that it is possible to increase the representation of Black men in leadership roles in urban public schools. By implementing targeted recruitment efforts, mentorship programs, leadership pipelines, and culturally responsive practices, schools and districts can create environments where Black male leaders can thrive. The following chapter will explore the long-term benefits of Black male leadership in education and how these leaders contribute to closing the achievement gap and improving outcomes for all students.

Chapter 8: The Long-Term Benefits of Black Male Leadership in Urban Schools

The underrepresentation of Black men in senior leadership positions in urban schools has been shown to have negative effects on both school culture and student outcomes. However, when

Black men are elevated to leadership roles, the benefits extend far beyond the individual school, contributing to the long-term success of the students, the schools, and the communities they serve. This chapter will explore the various ways in which Black male leadership positively impacts the education system, with a particular focus on closing the achievement gap, improving school climate, and fostering a culture of inclusivity.

8.1. Closing the Achievement Gap

One of the most significant benefits of Black male leadership in urban schools is its potential to help close the achievement gap between students of color and their white peers. Research has shown that Black male leaders are more likely to implement culturally responsive teaching practices and curricula that reflect the lived experiences of students of color . These leaders understand the importance of connecting academic content to students' cultural backgrounds, which has been shown to improve engagement and academic achievement.

For example, schools led by Black male principals often see increases in graduation rates and college enrollment for students of color. These leaders advocate for high academic expectations while also providing the support systems necessary to help students succeed. Black male leaders are more likely to implement mentoring programs, after-school tutoring, and college preparation workshops that specifically target students of color, ensuring that they have the resources needed to excel academically .

In addition to improving academic outcomes for Black students, Black male leaders also help bridge the gap for other marginalized student groups, including Latino and immigrant students. By fostering a school environment that values diversity and inclusion, Black male leaders create opportunities for all students to thrive, regardless of their background.

8.2. Reducing Disciplinary Disparities

Black male leadership has been shown to play a key role in reducing disciplinary disparities, particularly for Black male students, who are disproportionately subjected to harsh disciplinary measures such as suspensions and expulsions. Schools with Black male leaders are more likely to adopt restorative justice practices, which focus on conflict resolution and relationship-building rather than punitive measures .

Restorative justice practices have been shown to reduce suspensions and improve student behavior by addressing the root causes of conflict and providing students with the tools they need to manage their emotions and resolve disputes peacefully. Black male leaders, who often have firsthand experience with the challenges faced by students of color, are uniquely positioned to implement these practices in a way that resonates with students.

For example, schools that have implemented restorative justice under the leadership of Black male principals have seen significant reductions in suspensions and expulsions for Black male students, as well as improved overall school climate . By fostering an environment where students feel supported rather than criminalized, Black male leaders help break the school-to-prison pipeline and ensure that students remain engaged in their education.

8.3. Improving School Climate and Student Engagement

School climate plays a critical role in student success, and Black male leaders have been shown to positively influence school climate by creating an environment where all students feel valued and supported. Research has shown that students perform better academically and socially when they feel connected to their school community, and Black male leaders are more likely to foster this sense of connection by building strong relationships with students, staff, and parents .

Black male leaders often serve as role models for students of color, particularly Black boys, who may not see themselves reflected in other areas of society. By providing students with a positive example of leadership and success, Black male principals help students envision a future where they can achieve their goals. This sense of possibility is critical for student engagement, as students who see themselves reflected in their school leaders are more likely to take ownership of their education and actively participate in school activities .

In addition to improving student engagement, Black male leaders also contribute to a more inclusive school climate by advocating for policies and practices that support the needs of marginalized students. For example, Black male leaders are more likely to implement inclusive curricula, culturally responsive teaching practices, and programs that address the mental health and well-being of students of color. These initiatives help create a school environment where all students feel welcome and supported, leading to improved academic and social outcomes.

8.4. Fostering a Culture of Inclusivity and Diversity

The presence of Black male leaders in urban schools also helps foster a culture of inclusivity and diversity, which benefits both students and staff. Schools with diverse leadership teams are more likely to implement policies and practices that reflect the needs of their diverse student populations. This includes everything from hiring a more diverse teaching staff to offering professional development on cultural competency and anti-racism.

Black male leaders often prioritize the creation of inclusive school environments where all students, regardless of their background, can thrive. This includes advocating for equitable access to resources, such as advanced coursework, extracurricular activities, and college preparation programs. It also involves addressing systemic barriers that may prevent students of color from fully participating in the school community, such as discriminatory disciplinary practices or a lack of culturally relevant curricula .

In addition to benefiting students, fostering a culture of inclusivity and diversity also has positive effects on staff. Black male leaders who prioritize diversity in hiring are more likely to create a supportive work environment for teachers of color, which can improve teacher retention and job satisfaction. Research has shown that teachers of color are more likely to stay in schools where they feel supported by a diverse leadership team . By creating an inclusive work environment, Black male leaders help ensure that schools can attract and retain talented educators who are committed to serving diverse student populations.

8.5. Building Stronger Community Ties

Black male leaders are often deeply connected to the communities they serve, and their leadership can help strengthen the relationship between schools and their surrounding communities. Research shows that schools with strong community ties tend to have better student outcomes, including higher attendance rates, lower dropout rates, and improved academic performance .

Black male leaders, who often share the cultural backgrounds of their students and families, are uniquely positioned to build trust and engage the community in meaningful ways. This may include hosting community forums, partnering with local organizations to provide wraparound services for students, and creating opportunities for parents to become actively involved in their children's education.

By building stronger community ties, Black male leaders help create a sense of shared ownership and investment in the success of the school. This sense of community not only benefits students but also fosters a more positive school climate, where staff, students, and families work together to achieve common goals.

8.6. Role Modeling and Aspiration Building for Future Leaders

Another long-term benefit of Black male leadership is the role modeling it provides for future generations of leaders. Black male students who see themselves reflected in school leadership are more likely to aspire to leadership roles themselves, creating a positive feedback loop that helps increase the representation of Black men in education over time.

By serving as visible examples of success, Black male leaders inspire students of color to pursue careers in education and leadership. This is particularly important in urban schools, where students of color may not see many professionals who share their backgrounds. The presence of Black male leaders helps students envision a future where they can achieve their goals and make meaningful contributions to their communities .

Mentorship is a key component of this aspiration-building process. Black male leaders who mentor young men of color provide them with the guidance, support, and encouragement they need to pursue leadership opportunities. These mentorship relationships help build confidence and leadership skills, ensuring that future generations of Black men are prepared to take on leadership roles in education and beyond.

8.7. Conclusion

The long-term benefits of Black male leadership in urban schools are clear. From closing the achievement gap and reducing disciplinary disparities to improving school climate and fostering a culture of inclusivity, Black male leaders have a transformative impact on the education system. Their presence not only benefits students but also strengthens the school community and helps create a more equitable and inclusive education system for all. The final chapter will present policy recommendations and a call to action for educators, policymakers, and communities to continue working toward increasing the representation of Black men in leadership roles.

Chapter 9: Policy Recommendations and a Call to Action

The underrepresentation of Black men in senior leadership roles within urban public schools has been well-documented throughout this book. It is evident that Black male leaders have a transformative impact on school culture, student achievement, and community engagement. However, addressing the challenges they face requires intentional, comprehensive strategies that engage multiple stakeholders, including policymakers, school districts, educators, and communities. This final chapter presents policy recommendations and a call to action aimed at increasing the representation of Black men in school leadership roles. The recommendations are divided into three levels: local, state, and federal.

9.1. Local Government and School District Recommendations

At the local level, school districts and municipal governments have a critical role to play in ensuring that Black male educators have the support they need to ascend into leadership roles. These recommendations focus on recruitment, retention, mentorship, and accountability within local schools.

9.1.1. Establish Targeted Recruitment and Retention Programs

Local school districts should establish targeted recruitment programs specifically designed to attract Black men to leadership positions. These programs should include outreach to historically Black colleges and universities (HBCUs), professional organizations, and community-based networks to actively seek out Black male candidates for administrative roles.

Additionally, retention strategies are essential for keeping Black men in the profession once they enter leadership roles. These strategies should include:

9 **Competitive compensation** packages that reflect the experience and contributions of Black male leaders.

10 **Professional development opportunities** focused on leadership skills, cultural competency, and equity in education.

11 **Leadership coaching** and mentorship programs that provide ongoing support for Black male leaders as they navigate the challenges of school administration.

9.1.2. Implement School Leadership Pipelines

School districts should implement leadership pipeline programs that provide Black male educators with clear, structured pathways to leadership roles. These pipelines should offer leadership training, hands-on administrative experience, and mentorship from experienced school leaders. Leadership pipelines can begin as early as the teacher recruitment phase, with districts identifying potential leaders among their teaching staff and providing them with the tools they need to advance.

By establishing these leadership pipelines, school districts can create a sustainable pipeline of Black male leaders who are prepared to take on the challenges of school administration. These programs should also prioritize culturally responsive leadership training, ensuring that future leaders are equipped to meet the needs of diverse student populations.

9.1.3. Prioritize Culturally Responsive Leadership

Local governments and school districts should prioritize culturally responsive leadership at all levels of the education system. This includes offering professional development workshops and training sessions on cultural competency, anti-racism, and equity. School boards and hiring committees should receive training on implicit bias and equitable hiring practices to ensure that Black male candidates are evaluated fairly.

In addition to professional development, school districts should ensure that culturally responsive leadership is a core component of their leadership evaluation systems. School leaders should be assessed on their ability to create inclusive, equitable environments for students and staff, and districts should provide support to help leaders develop these skills.

9.1.4. Establish Accountability Systems for Diversity in Leadership

School districts should establish accountability systems that track the racial and gender diversity of their leadership teams. These systems should include regular reporting on the representation of Black men in leadership roles, as well as data on student outcomes, disciplinary practices, and teacher retention rates. By collecting and analyzing this data, districts can identify disparities and take action to address them.

Incentives can be provided for schools and districts that demonstrate significant progress in increasing the representation of Black men in leadership roles. These incentives could include additional funding for diversity initiatives, grants for professional development, and public recognition of schools that have successfully increased diversity in leadership.

9.2. State Government Recommendations

State governments have the power to enact policies that promote equity in school leadership across entire regions. These recommendations focus on state-level policy changes that can support Black male educators in their pursuit of leadership roles.

9.2.1. Mandate Diversity Training for Hiring Committees

State governments should mandate diversity training for all members of school hiring committees involved in the selection of principals, superintendents, and other administrative roles. This training should focus on reducing implicit bias and ensuring that Black male candidates are given fair consideration during the hiring process.

Additionally, states can establish guidelines for equitable hiring practices in schools and require districts to demonstrate compliance with these guidelines. By implementing these mandates, states can help ensure that school districts are actively working to increase the diversity of their leadership teams.

9.2.2. Provide Financial Incentives for Leadership Development

State governments should provide financial incentives to encourage Black male educators to pursue advanced degrees in educational leadership. These incentives could include scholarships, loan forgiveness programs, and leadership development grants that cover the cost of graduate-level coursework. By reducing the financial burden associated with obtaining leadership credentials, states can help increase the number of Black men who are prepared to take on administrative roles.

Additionally, state governments should consider providing stipends or salary increases for Black male educators who take on leadership roles in high-need urban schools. These financial incentives can help address the economic disparities that often prevent Black men from pursuing leadership positions.

9.2.3. Establish Statewide Leadership Development Programs

State governments should collaborate with universities and school districts to establish statewide leadership development programs that specifically target Black male educators. These programs should offer leadership training, mentorship, and opportunities for hands-on administrative experience. States can also partner with nonprofit organizations and professional associations to provide additional support for participants in these programs.

By offering statewide leadership development opportunities, states can create a larger pool of qualified Black male candidates for school leadership roles. These programs should prioritize culturally responsive leadership training and include a focus on equity, community engagement, and restorative justice practices.

9.2.4. Track and Report on Diversity in School Leadership

State departments of education should require school districts to report on the racial and gender diversity of their leadership teams, as well as student outcomes, disciplinary practices, and teacher retention rates. This data should be made publicly available and used to hold school districts accountable for their progress toward equity goals.

State governments can also create incentive programs that reward districts for making significant progress in increasing the representation of Black men in leadership roles. These incentives could include additional funding for diversity initiatives, public recognition, and grants for professional development.

9.3. Federal Government Recommendations

At the federal level, the Department of Education can play a key role in promoting equity in school leadership. These recommendations focus on federal policies and initiatives that can help increase the representation of Black men in leadership roles across the country.

9.3.1. Expand Federal Funding for Diversity Initiatives

The federal government should expand funding for diversity initiatives that support Black male educators in ascending to leadership roles. This could include grants for leadership development programs, scholarships for educators pursuing advanced degrees, and funding for mentorship and professional development opportunities. The Department of Education can also provide additional funding to districts that successfully increase the representation of Black men in leadership roles.

Additionally, the federal government should offer competitive grants to school districts that implement innovative strategies for recruiting and retaining Black male leaders. These grants could support initiatives such as leadership pipelines, culturally responsive leadership training, and restorative justice programs.

9.3.2. Establish National Standards for Diversity in School Leadership

The federal government should establish national standards for diversity in school leadership, ensuring that all school districts are working toward equitable representation in their leadership teams. These standards should include guidelines for recruiting, hiring, and retaining Black male leaders, as well as recommendations for addressing implicit bias and promoting culturally responsive leadership practices.

The Department of Education can provide technical assistance to school districts that are struggling to meet these standards, offering support in the form of professional development resources, mentorship programs, and leadership development initiatives.

9.3.3. Collect and Report National Data on School Leadership Diversity

The federal government should collect and report national data on the racial and gender diversity of school leadership teams. This data should be used to identify disparities and track progress toward national equity goals. By collecting and analyzing this data, the Department of Education can hold school districts accountable for their efforts to increase diversity in leadership.

Additionally, the federal government should create a national recognition program that honors schools and districts that have made significant progress in increasing the representation of Black men in leadership roles. This recognition could include financial incentives, public awards, and opportunities for districts to share their successful strategies with other schools.

9.4. A Call to Action for Educators, Policymakers, and Communities

The underrepresentation of Black men in school leadership is not a problem that can be solved by any one group—it requires a collective effort from educators, policymakers, and communities. This section outlines specific actions that each group can take to help address this issue and create a more equitable education system.

9.4.1. Educators

Educators can play a key role in supporting the advancement of Black men into leadership roles by:

- **Mentoring and sponsoring Black male colleagues** who are interested in pursuing leadership positions.

- **Advocating for equitable hiring practices** and diversity in leadership within their schools and districts.
- **Participating in professional development** on cultural competency and implicit bias to ensure that they are creating inclusive environments for their colleagues and students.

9.4.2. Policymakers

Policymakers at the local, state, and federal levels can support equity in school leadership by:

- **Enacting policies that promote diversity in school leadership**, including targeted recruitment efforts, leadership development programs, and accountability systems.
- **Providing funding for diversity initiatives** that support Black male educators in pursuing leadership roles.
- **Establishing national and state standards for diversity in leadership**, and holding school districts accountable for meeting these standards.

9.4.3. Communities

Communities can support the advancement of Black men into leadership roles by:

- **Advocating for equitable representation** in school leadership within their local districts.

- **Engaging with schools and school leaders** to ensure that they are responsive to the needs of the community, particularly for students of color.

- **Supporting Black male educators** by participating in mentorship programs, offering community-based leadership development opportunities, and fostering partnerships between local organizations and schools.

- **Raising awareness** about the importance of Black male leadership in schools through local advocacy, media campaigns, and community forums.

9.5. Conclusion: The Future of Black Male Leadership in Education

The future of Black male leadership in urban public schools depends on our collective ability to dismantle the barriers that have historically prevented Black men from rising into positions of power and influence within the education system. By implementing the policy recommendations outlined in this chapter and taking deliberate, coordinated action at the local, state, and federal levels, we can create an education system that is more equitable, inclusive, and reflective of the diverse communities it serves.

Black male leaders are essential not only for improving student outcomes but for transforming the culture of our schools, fostering a sense of belonging and empowerment for all students, and ensuring that the voices and experiences of historically marginalized groups are represented in the decision-making processes that shape our education system. The journey to increasing Black male leadership in education requires a sustained commitment from all stakeholders, but the potential rewards—for students, schools, and society as a whole—are immeasurable.

The time for action is now. By creating pathways to leadership, providing the necessary support and resources, and holding ourselves accountable for the outcomes, we can ensure that future generations of students have the opportunity to learn and grow in environments where Black male leaders are not the exception, but the norm.

Summation

The underrepresentation of Black men in senior leadership positions within urban public schools is not just an issue of diversity—it is a critical factor affecting the quality and equity of education for countless students, particularly those from marginalized communities. Throughout this book, we have explored the deep-rooted historical barriers, the systemic biases, and the missed opportunities that contribute to the alienation of Black men from leadership roles. We have also examined the profound impact that Black male leaders have on improving student outcomes, transforming school culture, and bridging the gap between schools and their communities.

The urgency of addressing these disparities cannot be overstated. Black male leaders bring a unique set of experiences, perspectives, and cultural competencies that are essential for fostering inclusive, supportive, and academically rigorous learning environments. Their leadership not only benefits Black male students, who often lack role models within the education system, but also contributes to the overall success and equity of schools.

However, solving this issue requires a collective commitment from educators, policymakers, and communities. It requires targeted recruitment and leadership pipelines, mentorship programs, and policy changes at every level—local, state, and federal. Most importantly, it requires a shift in how we view leadership in education, recognizing that representation, inclusivity, and equity are foundational to building strong, effective schools.

The way forward is clear, but it will take sustained effort and intentional actions to ensure that Black men are no longer alienated from leadership roles in our schools. By addressing the systemic barriers and fostering pathways to leadership, we can create an education system that reflects the diversity and potential of its students.

It is time to take action, and together, we can build a future where Black men are at the forefront of educational leadership, guiding the next generation toward success, equity, and empowerment.

Works Cited

Anderson, M. D. (2020). *A Seat at the Table: Black Educators' Strategies for School Leadership.* Harvard Education Review.

Achinstein, B., & Ogawa, R. T. (2011). *Change(d) Agents: New Teachers of Color in Urban Schools.* Teachers College Press.

Brown, A. L. (2009). "Brothers Empowered to Teach: The Role of Mentorship in Recruiting and Retaining Men of Color in Urban Schools." *Journal of African American Males in Education.*

Carter, P. L. (2005). *Keepin' It Real: School Success Beyond Black and White.* Oxford University Press.

Darling-Hammond, L. (2010). *The Flat World and Education: How America's Commitment to Equity Will Determine Our Future.* Teachers College Press.

Fenning, P., & Rose, J. (2007). "Overrepresentation of African American Students in Exclusionary Discipline: The Role of School Policy." *Urban Education.*

Gay, G. (2010). *Culturally Responsive Teaching: Theory, Research, and Practice*. Teachers College Press.

Gershenson, S., Hart, C. M., Lindsay, C. A., & Papageorge, N. W. (2017). "The Long-Run Impacts of Same-Race Teachers." *National Bureau of Economic Research*.

Gollnick, D. M., & Chinn, P. C. (2017). *Multicultural Education in a Pluralistic Society*. Pearson Education.

Howard, T. C. (2014). *Black Male(d): Peril and Promise in the Education of African American Males*. Teachers College Press.

Ishimaru, A. M. (2013). "From Heroes to Organizers: Principals and Education Organizing in Urban School Reform." *Educational Administration Quarterly*.

Johnson, L. (2006). "Making Her Community a Better Place to Live: Culturally Responsive Urban School Leadership in Historical Context." *Leadership and Policy in Schools*.

Khalifa, M. A. (2018). *Culturally Responsive School Leadership*. Harvard Education Press.

Ladson-Billings, G. (1994). *The Dreamkeepers: Successful Teachers of African American Children.* Jossey-Bass.

Milner, H. R. (2015). *Start Where You Are, But Don't Stay There: Understanding Diversity, Opportunity Gaps, and Teaching in Today's Classrooms.* Harvard Education Press.

National Association of Secondary School Principals. (2020). *Diversity and Inclusion in School Leadership.* NASSP Bulletin.

Noguera, P. A. (2003). *City Schools and the American Dream: Reclaiming the Promise of Public Education.* Teachers College Press.

Pollock, M. (2004). *Colormute: Race Talk Dilemmas in an American School.* Princeton University Press.

Skiba, R. J., Arredondo, M. I., & Rausch, M. K. (2014). "Discipline Disparities: A Research-to-Practice Collaborative." *The Equity Project at Indiana University.*

Tatum, B. D. (2017). *Why Are All the Black Kids Sitting Together in the Cafeteria?: And Other Conversations About Race.* Basic Books.

Tillman, L. C. (2004). "African American Principals and Leadership: History and Significance in African American Schools." *Educational Administration Quarterly*.

Walker, V. S. (2009). *Hello Professor: A Black Principal and Professional Leadership in the Segregated South*. University of North Carolina Press.

Wright, B. L., & Counsell, S. (2018). "The Kids Are Alright: Deepening Black Male Students' Engagement in the Study of African American History." *Journal of Urban Learning, Teaching, and Research*.